BEST RELATIONSHIP ADVICES FOR COUPLES

DR. FEMI "GFEM" OGUNJINMI

Published by:
Light Switch Press
PO Box 272847
Fort Collins, CO 80527

Copyright © 2021

ISBN: 978-1-953284-47-1

Printed in the United States of America

(1)   Love is strong medicine. If you took it for the wrong person, you will be sad and broken. But if you took it for the right person, you will be glad and whole.

(2)   Ladies, it is okay to want a guy who has nice pockets but beware of a guy who spends money on you versus the one who invests in you; the one who views you properly than a property. They can be distinctively two different men.

(3)   When people say they have been married for a long time to earn some respect, I simply ask, are you happy in the relationship? It does not matter how long the relationship has been existing. It is about being happy in the relationship. It is not about the quantity but the quality of the relationship. Do not live for numbers; live for non-tangible happiness that should be non-negotiable.

(4)   People often explore Biology (sex) before Chemistry in their relationship. When they have conflict, they use sex as a method to resolve the conflict. However, the problem remains unfixed after the sex. It is imperative to build chemistry, understand how to communicate with one another so that when there is an issue, you can address it the right way.

(5)   Relationship is not something you hop from every few months or years like a job. There are feeling involved. Just because you see another job well advertised and

packaged nicely does not mean it is authentic and you are compatible with the company. Do not turn down what you have for a 20 who appears to be 80. Do your research well.

(6)   One of the bad attitudes that ruin a relationship is that we spend too much time telling our partners what we dislike about them instead of what we like about them. Can you just take few minutes today and celebrate with your partner? Express what you love about them, a particular character, gift, deed, any positive thing they do, maybe paying your child tuition, cooking, helping with the chores, fasting, and praying over the family, holding the family down when you are not around or when you are physically ill.

(7)   If you have a low opinion of yourself, you will be walked over in your relationship if you are with a partner who does not care about your feelings. I encourage you to pick yourself up (self-esteem)   and raise your head high. Have self-worth, self-value, and high confidence in yourself.

(8)   God's factor is a sine qua non in the process of relationship. Without God's hand in your marriage, it will not be as smooth as it is supposed to be.

(9)   You cannot force someone to love you just like you cannot force a horse to drink water. The more you force that

person the more he or she withdraws emotionally and physically.

(10) Most men are not smart enough to realize the more you elevate your woman, the less available and accessible she is for other men. But when you put her down and belittle her, you make her accessible to anyone she thinks will treat her right and better.

(11) Men should learn to say I love you frequently to their partner. The statement "I love you" is not only said when you are trying to woo the person. It is a repetitive word that should be said every day to your partner (even to your children). Another thing is to cultivate holding hands in public, put your hands around your partner, and show affection. Let her feel loved. Women are moved by what they hear. They can complain of everything else but can never complain hearing that statement, "I love you."

(12) Bible says a man will leave his mother and father and cleave to his wife. The difference between leaving and cleaving is "C" and that stands for Christ. Invite Christ to your relationship and let him be your foundation.

(13) One of the best ways to earn brownie points from your partner (especially your wife) is to help them do some chores without them asking you to do it.

(14) It is hard to work on other important elements of the relationship when the physical attraction is not there. Attraction is a prelude to a relationship. The absence of it can be a detriment to a successful relationship.

(15) If you are not ready to be wrong and correct, then you are not ready for a real relationship.

(16) For all the newlyweds and those that are about to get married, remember when you say yes on the altar, best believe it that you say yes to a lot of unforeseen things.

(17) One stage in a relationship that requires consistent hard work is Maintenance! It comes after the honeymoon phase has fizzled out. It is a stage that consumes the most resources. Finding out your mistakes, working on yourself, preventing yourself from performing damaging actions, building thick skin, communicating effectively, understanding your partner, strengthening your intimacy, cultivating positive habits, talking every day, and fighting right.

(18) Forgiveness is maturity! It is for people with a big heart.

(19) The difference between our women today and the ones back in the days is that more women speak up today in their relationship; they convey what they want and dislike. There is nothing wrong with your lady speaking up. She is just being expressive.

(20) Sex is a physical communion with your partner. Talking is an emotional and mental communion with your partner. You should not like one over the other. You got to enjoy doing both and stop complaining your partner talks too much. How about you listen too much.

(21) You can tell a woman loves you when her friends say you are no good, but she ignores them by holding on to the word you said to her, "I love you."

(22) Husband and wife should always work together like a pair of scissors. Anything that comes between them should be cut off. For what God has joined together, let no man put asunder.

(23) Husbands when it comes to sex, show how loving and caring you are and not how fast you can release. It is imperative to put your wife's needs ahead of yours and practice self-control.

(24) One of the powerful tools we possess is our tongue. It can make or break us. Be careful how you use your tongue to talk to your partner. Elevate and not bash each other with your tongue. People do not forget the horrible things you say to them.

(25) Why we do not enjoy our partner at times is because we zero in on their bad behavior(s)   and overlook other areas they are good for. There is more to a person than

the one bad character you see. Learn to flip to their good character just like you flip to the next chapter of a book.

(26) Most of us never really knew ourselves before the commitment and which is causing so much drama in our relationships. Perhaps you knew yourself does not mean you will not learn a thing or two when you get in a relationship. Do not stop learning and growing. You are responsible for your actions. If you stop learning and growing, you will kill your relationship.

(27) It is a wrong idea to invest thousands of dollars and time into planning a wedding that lasts few days and invest nothing into a marriage you are expecting to last a lifetime

(28) You cannot abuse your wife and still expect the blessings of Proverbs 18:22 (He who finds a wife finds a good thing and obtains favor from God). Your wife's tears will block God's ears from answering your prayers.

(29) Once you can show a woman you are worth listening to, submitting to, and capable of leading, she will fall deeply in love and do all you say.

(30) Don't be a liability in your relationship. Be an asset. Always contributing and bringing something to the table. A liability has nothing to bargain for and no voice.

(31) On the note on sex to wives: it is not every time you should be down (missionary). Bible says thou shall not be beneath...Change your position, come up, look your husband in the eye, watch his reaction, take the wheel, and drive both of you to the destination.

(32) Men, don't allow the serpent to talk to your wife. Be present, Be sensitive, and Be in control. Do not abdicate your responsibility. The mistake of Adam was that he was not present and accountable. God will always look at you first when things go wrong because He puts you in charge of the household.

(33) If the foundation is solid and you know how to water it, marriage should be one of the best decisions of your life and not the worst.

(34) My mom set an example of what a woman should be by her characters. I studied her while growing up and I told myself, I want a woman with the same morals. Dear wives, as you grow in your relationship, always remember your son will want to use you as a point of reference for the woman he wants to marry. You can either be a good reference or a bad reference. The same goes for men that are becoming fathers: Set the example of the kind of man you want your daughter(s)   to marry.

(35) If you do not like what you are receiving from your partner, then change what you are giving.

(36) A relationship where you both think and do things for one another is bound to last.

(37) If where you leave in the morning and sleep in the evening is peaceful, then it does not matter what happens during the day because you will always start and end your day with peace. Make your home peaceful.

(38) Relationship is not about what the outside culture says; it's about the culture you develop in your relationship. Do not be influenced by traditions. Create your own culture that works for both of you.

(39) If partners want their relationship to be as successful as bad as they want to breathe, they will get the result they want by doing all the necessary step it takes.

(40) Just like a wedding ring is round with no end, your marriage should be the same. Nothing should come in between to break it except death.

(41) Only hurt people hurt people. Only unhappy people make others unhappy.

(42) There is one common issue I see with those in a relationship and that is "Happiness." Everyone wants to be happy and looking for that one person for the job. When you live a life waiting for others to make you happy, you become vulnerable and not always satisfied. What you

need to do is to tap into your internal happiness and that will change the outcome of your love life.

(43) Husbands, when last have you showed affection to your wives? As of lately have you tickled, kissed, held, pecked, or carried her as you did on your wedding day? Do not let the baby weight on your wife be an excuse. You too go and lift weight so that you can carry her.

(44) When a woman gets older, she is still attracted to that bad rough guy you were once that she met. She still wants you to talk dirty to her. Just because you are married with kids does not stop you from keeping it funky and turning up. Just make sure you only turn up with her alone. Do not dull yourself. Satisfy her!!!

(45) Inability to forgive one another, leaves no room for growth. Without forgiveness, we really cannot move on. It is hard to forgive but it is the best thing to do.

(46) Don't get disappointed when you are engaged to someone under 25yrs of age and he or she is acting immature and making irrational decisions. Science says your brain is not fully formed until you are 25yrs old.

(47) Sometimes in life you have to drop the zero and get with a hero. Other times, it's best to help make the zero an hero. May God give you the spirit of discernment to know who you are with and what decision to make.

(48) Do not use each other's weakness to pull each other and destroy one another. Rather use it to lift and strengthen each other.

(49) The best part about love is fighting through your disagreement/argument quickly and bouncing back to a peaceful state again.

(50) Spend more time with your partner and less time alone or with other people. Your relationship requires time together to deepen your love and increase your understanding of each other. What you spend time most is what you know.

(51) Don't create a problem by trying to solve a problem. For example: walking out on each other during an argument can lead to an accident on your way out or lead to falling in the hands of someone else.

(52) Don't marry a man because he has a television. Marry a man because he can tell you his vision, you can see yourself in his vision, and eventually, you will both have the television.

(53) If you are not ready to make the sacrifice then you are not ready to be in a relationship, talk less about becoming a parent. Sacrifice is one of the key requirements of becoming a partner and parent. Learn to make a sacrifice

now and then if you want to experience the latent joy, peace, and longevity of the relationship.

(54) Many are suffering in a relationship because of the bad decision they made years ago or recently. That decision is hunting and hurting their relationship. The choice we make becomes our foundation. Everything builds on it and cascades from there.

(55) Me, Mine, and I - The trinity that destroys a relationship. I want this, I want that, it is my money, it is my house, or it is my car. Stay away from that mindset and phrases. They will negatively affect your relationship. Everything you own in a relationship belongs to both of you. Two shall be joined together and become one.

(56) 3 Big C's that might be missing in your relationship: Creativity, Commitment, & Conversation. Work on these pillars and your relationship will be rock solid.

(57) Marriage has nothing to do with age but maturity. Though maturity most time comes with age, people who are old are sometimes as confused as young people. Jesus says not everyone is matured enough to live a married life. He did not put an age on it. Adam and Eve were created as matured beings (Genesis 2:22-24)   to depict the profile of marriage and that is a reason God did not spare them of consequences for not following his instructions.

Check your relationship if you are not making mature decisions.

(58) 3 Habits of a successful relationship: (a) B a l a n c e your work, spiritual, and other facets of life with your partner (b) Support each other (c) Do not take each other for granted.

(59) Many are experiencing fiery trials in their relationship and they are hoping for a fairy tale. The attributed cause of the problem is that people marry to love and not love to marry. Do not be in a rush for marriage if love is not present. Hoping to find love when you get married is wishful thinking. It is good to be proactive. Your foundation of love can help you get through difficult times in the relationship. But if love never existed, you would wish to leave the relationship.

(60) A relationship built on lies and fakery is bound for a lot of troubles. If the car, house, money, clothes, job profession, job title, or other accomplishments are not yours, then do not claim them. Telling someone that you have what you do not have is pure lies.

(61) Marriage is not an idealistic union for perfect beings but a realistic and complementary relationship where everyone has his/her strengths/weakness. For this reason, there should be no competition, envy, or jealousy between the couple. But with collaboration, there will

be peace, joy, and a lot of accomplishments. Make that your goal.

(62) People who come to your life are either a blessing or a lesson. Whatever they choose to be is for your benefit, growth, and endurance. Never feel down or disappointed for anything. Just keep it moving.

(63) If you are happy your wife is not giving you trouble and you have peace in your home, it is bound for you to be successful. And that is also if you are not lazy. The bible says he who has found a wife obtains favor from God.

(64) Just the fact that you are angry at each other and not in a good mood or space with another should not stop your responsibility as a husband and wife.

(65) Women are emotional beings, and their sexuality is connected to their emotions. If you want to have sex with your wife, it is important to cater to her emotions. Set her mood in the right direction from morning till the time you want to have the action.

(66) If you plan to break up with your partner that means one or a combination of these things has taken place: (a) the love you once had is gone (b) there is something more powerful than the love you had that is tearing the relationship apart (c) there was no love from the beginning of the relationship, to begin with.

(67) Work might be stressful, the job may be a loss, the business might be crashing, you might be failing classes, money might be tough, your critics might be blaming you, bills may be difficult to pay but when you come home and you have a partner that makes you forget the issues and provide support, that is when you know you've got the right partner.

(68) Your relationship is not beyond repair. It is either one or two of these things that are happening (a)   You have or have not discovered the solution (b)   You do not want to repair it.

(69) It is not about how much you fight but how well you learn from your fight that you can prevent the same fight again.

(70) Three daily habits of successful couples: Pray together, Play together, & Plan together.

(71) If you are still angry, bitter, and disappointed about your past relationship then you cannot successfully handle a brand-new relationship with satisfaction, happiness, peace, and excitement.

(72) You must be in a relationship with someone willing to do for you as much as you are willing to do in return. A relationship is a two-way street.

(73) Don't close your eyes on your relationship. Even though it is not perfect (Just like any other relationship), you can still find contentment with what is right and satisfactory in it.

(74) Even if you do not have sex with each other often, do not forget to always flirt and give each other sexy compliments. It will improve your intimacy and help to stay connected emotionally, physically, and mentally.

(75) When you satisfy the requirements at home first, you will feel happy, energized, and confident to satisfy the requirements in the world. When the home is good, every other thing is approachable and doable.

(76) Relationship is like a living document. There is always some update and modification to it. Keep fixing and updating your relationship.

(77) A successful relationship is not the result of one act of service. It is the repetition and consistent service you provide to one another that gives the result you desire.

(78) No matter how old or young your relationship is, you still need to continue watering it if you want it to stay alive. Because no matter how old a tree is, it still needs water to stay alive and survive.

(79) Pledge daily to be faithful to your relationship. Do not be a faith-fool!

(80) The more time you spend together, the better you understand each other and reduce conflicts. People grow apart because they do not spend time together. You can be living in the same house and still grow apart because you are not spending time together.

(81) Your home should be heaven on earth. If your heart is always pounding hoping she is asleep before you get home, hoping he is not home to beat you up, thinking he or she should just sign the divorce paper, then your home is not heaven on earth.

(82) The combination of a man who lacks wisdom and patience and a woman who lacks good manners and cannot control her mouth will damage their relationship.

(83) Can the two work together except they agree? A successful relationship is a result of two determined people to make it work.

(84) Wives, your husbands do not want sex, they need it just like a car needs gasoline to run. Make sure your gas station stays open and only serve "Premium service". Not regular or mid-grade.

(85) If you are okay being naked in the bedroom with your spouse then you should be okay being naked about your money, investment, accounts, how much you are getting back in tax returns, etc. You should not hide your assets

and plans from each other. That is the true essence of becoming "One flesh."

(86) You were worth something when you met each other; you had a price tag. Has your tag price reduced or increased since then? Do not be like an item of clothing on sale: it was $100 before now it is $10. Increase your price tag. Improve yourself in different facets of life.

(87) With or without marriage, you should still become who God has destined you to become. Do not let marriage be your destination.

(88) If you let anger control you, it can destroy all you have worked hard for including your relationship. Control it do not let it control you.

(89) Instead of looking for a new partner to love, why don't you look for new ways to love the one you have.

(90) Marriage is to be enjoyed and not endured! Though there might be a little endurance, it should not last forever. Weeping may endure for a night, but joy comes in the morning.

(91) Do not deprive your partner of intimacy for that long because you are fasting. When you break make sure you become intimate. Balance your spiritual and married life. "Do not deprive one another except with consent for a time, that you may give yourselves to fasting and

prayer; and come together again so that Satan does not tempt you because of your lack of self-control." 1 Corinthians 7:5.

(92) If you expect your man to know what you need & want at your desire time, well, well, well, he is not God. He is man-made of clay. He does not know what is in your mind. Just communicate what you want and need. Keep the situation simple!

(93) Know who you marry, respect what you marry, love what you marry, and support what you marry.

(94) To satisfy him, you try to change how you dress, put on nice lingerie, put on make-up, compete with the kinky girls out there and he still does not see you. Well, I do not think he is blind. He has lost interest.

(95) You want a guy who makes six figures and then he turns around and spends the money on other girls. You want a man who has a six-pack, well built, and then he boxes you like iron Mike Tyson. There is nothing wrong with having a man with money and a nice physique but there is more to superficial things when it comes to being in a healthy and satisfying relationship.

(96) Your husband does not want to struggle to reach that precious thing. Going to bed with 2-3 layers of clothes kills the action. Keep yourself easily accessible to your

partner in your bedroom. You were made naked and naked ye shall return.

(97) It hurts a woman when she is not carried along in decision-making in the house. She feels as though she is irrelevant, and you do not regard her.

(98) You need to become a complete, independent person before and while you are in a relationship otherwise you will become a burden.

(99) There are different types of love. The one we most think of Eros: it's the sexual love that is most akin to our modern construct of romantic love. This kind of love does not last and is based on so many conditions and self-interest (i.e looks, money, care, respect, etc.) The only type of love that is most important and will last is Agape love (unconditional love). It is based on zero conditions. If couples have that for one another, they will be able to prevent/and or endure all things.

(100) Women are more emotional beings and sensitive than men while men are more on the analytical side. Therefore, you need to allow your woman to tell you how she is feeling. A woman can sense troubles from miles away. But for you as a man, even if the trouble is under your nose you may not feel it.

(101) All men are dogs as they say. If that is true, then you need yourself a trained one who listens and obeys his master (God). You need a good dog who will not eat everything he sees because all he sees is in one thing that he eats.

(102) Men need to realize that the reason sometimes their prayers are hindered is because they are busy disrespecting their wives. If a man's prayer is not being answered, he should first check how he is treating his wife because God will not answer a man's prayer who does not do right by his woman. 1Peter 3:7 "Husbands, in the same way, be considerate as you live with your wives and treat them with respect as the weaker partner and as heirs with you of the gracious gift of life so that nothing will hinder your prayers."

(103) The primary problem of relationships all over the world is that they operate relationship without information (Revelation). The operation of a thing without revelation (information) leads to frustration and destruction. Information begets operation.

(104) A healthy relationship is like eating something nutritious to be healthy. Quite often we do not like eating salad because we do not have a sense of taste for it, but we eat it regardless because we want to be healthy. So is relationship. There are right things you must do

in a relationship that you are not naturally inclined to do. But you must do them to make your relationship healthy.

(105) Don't experience madness in your relationship by doing the same thing and expecting to get a different result. If the old way is not working, then you need to switch up your strategy.

(106) If you get mad when your partner talks about his or her ex, then you probably not healed about what may have happened between your partner and the ex.

(107) If you cannot be satisfied by one person then no number of men or women can satisfy you. What you need is self-discipline, the Holy Spirit, and fear of God.

(108) If your definition of Mr. Right or Mrs. Right is a perfect person, sorry the person does not exist on this planet. What you might get is Mr. Almost Right or Ms. Pretty Close. God is the perfect one.

(109) A relationship is not about getting something from one another; it is about building something together.

(110) Improving your life automatically improves your relationship. Your relationship reflects who you are; If you and your partner can both grow together, your relationship will become a good by-product.

(111) You must be creative when it comes to sex with your partner. Having it just in the bedroom is boring.

(112) Having a complete true love is when the receiver is more like the giver.

(113) You need skills to build and maintain your relationship with your partner. Making love in the way your partner loves to requires skills.

(114) If you are not completing each other as a couple then you are depleting each other. There is no other way to it.

(115) Just because God made you the head of the family does not mean you should boss your wife around and not apologize when you are wrong.

(116) A relationship is one university you never graduate from. The moment you stop learning, the moment you stop growing.

(117) A man is indeed a provider. But not only so much about finances. A man should provide wisdom, ideas, the solution to problems, guidance, emotional intelligence, friendship, vision, camaraderie, mental toughness, and courage. The functionality of a man is way more than the bacon he brings home.

(118) He says he loves you during sex while you are mad at him does not mean he loves you at that moment. He just wants sex at that point.

(119) Every relationship is a work in progress. Keep working on it so that you can enjoy it.

(120) One effective principle to a successful and happy relationship is conversation. Arouse each other's mind and not just body. Have a dialogue and not a monologue.

(121) Submission is not what one person does in a relationship. It is what both parties do for one another as respect and honor to the commitment and viability of the marriage and ultimately to God who joined them together.

(122) Submission is not slavery. It is smartly putting your power under the control of another person for the goal of the relationship. You should always submit to one another to keep your relationship viable.

(123) What have you said to your partner lately? "A soothing tongue [speaking words that build up and encourage] is a tree of life, But a perverse tongue [speaking words that overwhelm and depress] crushes the spirit." Proverb 15:4 Amplified

(124) One non-physical fight or argument occasionally should not stop you from loving one another or quitting

your relationship. The fight does not mean your relationship is bad. It just shows that you guys still have more learning to do about each other. And it is better to learn than not to. Learning is part of your growth. If you are not learning, then you are not growing.

(125) Sex is one of the essential key components of marriage. If you are not pleasing each other in bed, not touching your partner the way you should, always finding an excuse not to be together then when are you going to enjoy your partner, or your partner enjoy you? I have not read that there will be love-making in heaven and when you die, someone else will enjoy your partner on earth.

(126) Every relationship has a problem. At the same time, it is important not to give power to the problem by talking too much about it. Be about the solution! When you study successful entrepreneurs and companies, they barely spend most of their time talking about problems; they invest most of their energy coming up with multiple solutions to fix the problem. If the solution you previously proposed does not work out, then strategize a new one. Do not stress your relationship with complaints. It will not get you anywhere. It will always push your partner away from you. Nobody wants to be around negative energy.

(127) Parents should understand that their children are learning about marriage by watching them. Therefore, avoid having serial arguments, domestic violence, cursing each other, and disrespect. If not, the children may think that is the norm and grow up being that way. Even accept such wrong behaviors from their future partner. The reality is that what we tolerate/reject from our partner or potential is mostly generated from past experiences we witnessed from our parents. If you want to prevent your children from having bad manners, choosing a bad partner, and being treated wrongly then it must start with you as parents treating each other better.

(128) Money cannot buy love, but it can make you enjoy love. The presence of money will make you discover another level of love for your partner. The absence of it can turn to serial arguments, anger, frustration, irritation, and annoyance.

(129) Any man who has no patience cannot enjoy his woman.

(130) You know how to be treated but you choose to be treated in the wrong way. Do not blame the person treating you badly. It is you accepting and tolerating the bad behavior. If you do not like what you are receiving, then change what you are giving.

(131) The challenge in a relationship is one person doing the right thing and the other doing the wrong thing. It will be good if it takes one person to make a good relationship. Unfortunately, it takes two people. Keep working on it.

(132) Holding hands, kissing, singing love songs, texting one another throughout the day, are great medicines to vitalize your union.

(133) If you did things that made you happy while you were single, why would you think your happiness is the sole responsibility of your partner while married? Your happiness is your sole responsibility in a relationship.

(134) It is okay to be imperfect. But it is paramount to work perfectly at your imperfections. It shows maturity and growth to your partner.

(135) Men enjoy respect just as much as women enjoy love. It is the DNA that cannot be altered. Give each other what is expected.

(136) Bringing up past mistake(s) of your partner that you have previously addressed can bring about conflict and destroy your relationship. If your reason for bringing up the past is because you want them to continue paying for their mistake, the question becomes for how long do you want the suffering to continue? The

mistake has been made and it cannot self-correct itself. Your lack of un-forgiveness and letting go will create a hostile environment in your relationship, which can make you lose your partner and relationship in the process.

(137) Hoping there will not be tough times in your relationship is wishful thinking. Your prayer is for God to give you strength, patience, understanding & wisdom to get through those tough times.

(138) A relationship of 1, 10, 20, or 30yrs can fail if the partners do not keep working on it. Gone at those days people stay in a relationship just for the sake of children or society views. Keep working on your relationship. Do not take each other for granted. Seek counseling if you need to.

(139) It is a great mistake when your woman has an issue and your first approach as a man is trying to solve it. Your first approach should be to listen with empathy. You need to first gain her trust that you care about her feelings, emotions and that you clearly understand what she is going through.

(140) 10% of conflict comes from the difference of opinion. The remaining 90 percent is from delivery and tonation. If you want to avoid the majority of the conflicts

in your relationship you will need to control the 90 percent.

(141) The reason you are not listening to each other during conflict is that you are both pointing fingers at each other without admitting first what you did to contribute to the problem and what you are going to do next time to prevent it from happening.

(142) There is a threshold to what a woman can take. If you keep playing with her heart she will just get up and leave your butt one day.

(143) Your wife is your AID and not your MAID. You cannot leave all responsibility for her.

(144) Whatever you demand, you should supply! If you demand food, supply the money for groceries. If you demand sex, you must be ready to warm her up. If you want her not to give you hell, then do not give her stress.

(145) Marriage is not a destination; It is a lifelong journey, and you must continually look for better ways to enjoy that ride with your spouse otherwise it will come to a halt.

(146) Give your partner a specific meaningful compliment. It will touch every fiber in their body to do more of what you just complimented them for.

(147) Do not make a permanent decision over a temporary situation. Beware of the devil that tries to trick you and whisper in your ears to break your relationship. Just because things are rough right now does not mean they will be like that forever. Every relationship has its challenging moment when it looks as if it is over, and the problem cannot be fixed. Just because your friend's relationship looks happy does not mean they have not had their tough moments. The emotions you are feeling will soon pass away like a cloud. Seek God and counseling.

(148) Do not put the burden of your happiness on your partner and do not let anyone make you feel responsible for their happiness. Their happiness is solely their responsibility.

(149) Know who you marry, respect who you marry, love who you marry, and support who you marry.

(150) If you love someone, you will make all the sacrifices to keep them. If you are not making the sacrifice, then it is either you do not love them, or your love is not deep enough. Do not fool around with him or her playing with your heart and head. If they are not making the sacrifice to correct their issues, bad behavior, and action then they are not in love with you, or the love is

just not deep enough to make the necessary changes to keep you.

(151) If your woman is mad at you that means she believed in you, but you broke her trust, and she is disappointed. If she is complaining and asking questions, it means she still cares. But if she is not talking and just allowing things to slide, that means she is giving up, or she has given up on you and possibly getting ready to leave your butt. Act before it gets to that moment.

(152) If you take your mind from always building and perfecting yourself, you will become a problem in the relationship. While you are in a relationship, it is important to exponentially develop yourself morally, academically, mentally, physically, financially, and spiritually.

(153) It is interesting what causes argument in a relationship when you expect your partner to magically get into your head and know exactly what should make you happy when you do not know what brings you happiness. Partners put too much expectation on each other, and it is a reflection that they do not fully understand themselves before getting into a relationship. Take time to know yourself, satisfy yourself, comfortable being with yourself, and loving yourself before deciding on spending your whole life with someone else. And if you are already married, still spend time know-

ing yourself. It will help you to communicate what you need to your partner.

(154) One of the integral components of a relationship is "Forgiveness." If you cannot forgive your partner and/or yourself, you are setting your relationship for failure. The end of a hardened heart is destruction. Ask Pharaoh! The Lord hardened his heart to lead him and his army to destruction at the Red Sea. What a sad ending. I do not wish the same for you. Have a forgiven heart.

(155) To have a great relationship, you need two things:

(a) The knowledge and tools to bring about the change you want. That is why reading books, getting coaching and attending seminars are important to acquire the knowledge that will shed light on your difficulties and give you the steps to overcome them.

(b) You need the drive to implement the acquired knowledge and make things work.

(156) Reminding your spouse constantly of what they do not do right is nagging. When you focus your attention on their flaws, you will be blind to see anything good about them, which will ultimately lead your mind to start seeing something good about another person outside your relationship. Focus your attention on the

good sides of your partner. Do not scorn them but encourage them.

(157) Bible says husbands should dwell with their wives according to knowledge. Unfortunately, men are dwelling with women according to the old knowledge of how the fathers/forefathers behaved towards their wives. Let me give you a new revelation: the landscape of relationships has drastically changed! If you do not play by the rules you will get replaced! Women are no longer staying in a relationship that is toxic, lacking care, sensitivity, and presence mixed with abuse and lackadaisical attitude. Do right by your woman; honor and care for her otherwise someone will replace your spot sexually, mentally, physically, and fatherly.

(158) You need to delay sex till y'all finish addressing the issues. Sex will not solve a problem that is not sex-related.

(159) People do not fall out of love; they usually fall out of forgiveness. When people break up over matters, it is typically they do not have any more energy and heart of forgiving the other person for their misbehavior(s).

(160) Sleep is for peace and not for pain. Resolve your matter with your partner before going to sleep.

(161) Communicate with your partner by (a) Validating their feelings; ask how they feel about what they are addressing you on (especially if they are dissatisfied with your action). (b) By regurgitating or paraphrasing to them what they say, suggests you are listening if indeed you were listening.

(162) Men should learn to exercise patience when interacting with their women. A man without patience cannot successfully enjoy his relationship. Same for women.

(163) The more I coach couples the more I realize everyone is becoming political in their conversation that is creating conflict. Yes, you have freedom of speech but do not just invoke it on your partner by being insensitive. If you want to get the best result from your conversation, you should speak with caution, respect, and tact otherwise your freedom of speech will create conflict and problems.

(164) Two of the strong factors that a Christian marriage requires to be viable are the Presence of God and Money. Money is a defense! When challenges of life offend you, you need money as a defense. And when the spiritual challenges of life offend you, you need the presence of God to defend you.

(165) The relationship culture of our generation is mistakenly focusing on trying to be like other couples and

less focus on knowing who we got married too! Let me make this a little bit clear... You desire and pressure your partner to do for you what someone else did for their partner or you often do things for your partner because others are doing it for their partner. Then you find out that your partner does not genuinely like what you do for them. You know why? because it is not what makes them feel appreciated and loved. You are not speaking their love language! Everyone has a love language such as words of affirmation, quality time, gift, an act of service, and physical touch. What needs to be done is to find your partner's love language, their uniqueness, and not others.

(166) If we can simplify our expectations there will be peace in our relationship. In other words, do not make your LOVE too expensive. It can lead your partner to frustration trying to satisfy and please you all the time. Eventually, they may withdraw. Recognize the ability and capacity of your spouse and meet them at that level. Perhaps you can strategically 'Work Together' to make life better.

(167) Everything that matters in life must be built. In other words, if something is important to you and want it to last, you must build it to last. Being in a relationship is just a title, but being in a successful relationship re-

quires "Work" that's not one day but years of commitment to building.

(168) Getting married is a track the society and culture have created for us as a symbolism of life progress. Either it is wrong or not, just do not let the pressure gets you to miss one of the important aspects of marriage: Enjoyment. If you are enjoying your single life or did enjoy your single life, your marriage should be a continuation of it. Not to say there will not be challenges. Perhaps you are enduring in your marriage, work with your partner and develop a course of action to fix it.

(169) Did you know God wants you to enjoy life with your wife? Bible says, "Enjoy life with the wife you love. Enjoy all the days of this short life God has given you here on earth. It is all you have. So, enjoy the work you have to do here on earth." Ecclesiastes 9:9 ICB

(170) It is good to be spiritual but doing it in the absence of not taking good care of yourself, not dressing the part, and looking all rough/unclean will make your partner find you undesired. Be spiritual and at the same time look attractive! You do not serve unclean God.

(171) The key to a sustained relationship is not in the love you had at the beginning of your relationship but in the continuous growth and renewing of that love. If your love tank is running low, you should revert to the prac-

tice of what you were doing in the old love (the way it used to be before the love ran low or out).

(172) We once used to be able to determine the fate, destiny of marriage from the onset of it by saying till death do us part. That means we know that marriage is over only when one of the couples dies or both. This time, we no longer can predict the destiny of marriage anymore. Death does not have to come before the marriage is broken. We create our death! The marriage of today is a marriage of hope! No assurance. keep hoping that it stays forever, last another day, weeks, months, years, and do not relent on doing what you are supposed to do.

(173) What's the number one activity any couple should do? It is not sex, not working out, not eating, nor sleeping. It is setting goals and plans for the family. People do not plan to fail; they fail to plan. Goals broken down in steps become plans and plans backed up with action becomes reality. If you want to succeed as a unit, sit down and develop goals you want your partner to work on and meet this year. Also vice versa. This also includes having goals for the children. Doing this will strengthen the bond of your relationship, bring you closer together, increase your understanding/communication, and overall create a harmonious relationship.

(174) The essence of being in a relationship is to spend so much time looking at each other and no time at other people.

(175) How do you satisfy, please, and bring happiness out of your partner? Big question but a simple response. ***Do what they complain about*** If she complains you do not come home on time, next time arrive on time. If he complains you do not make yourself available in the other room, next time make yourself available.

(176) An intimate Relationship is synonymous with a business relationship when it comes to communication. There is always negotiation happening. One of the general problems I see with couples is that the partners think their idea is the absolute best, so they want things to go their way by trying to win the other person to their side and they get upset and disappointed when they fail. Listen, do not expect the idea you came in with to be the one you will walk out with. Find a way to meet in the middle and derive the best solution for all. Next time you have a conversation with your partner, first have one with yourself and say, my idea may not be absolute; I am walking into this conversation to seek the best idea for us all. Remind yourself that every time and you will not be disappointed or left angry.

(177) I remember my wife and I went to eat at a restaurant and next to us was a family (husband, wife, and two kids). The kids must have been in their early teenage years. What caught our attention of this family and took us by surprise was that everyone was on their electronics (phone, iPad, headphone, etc.) and no one was talking to each other. The use of technology was creating a distance within them. Just like this family, the use of electronics and social media engagement create distance among couples and families. Know that when you are giving attention to electronics, social media, and the outside world, your spouse also needs attention, and they are far more important than any other thing. The first idea for you and your partner is to have an agreed time when you shut down all electronics, social media browsing, and communication with the outside world. The second idea is to be physically, mentally, and socially be present whenever your partner talks to you. Just pause what you are doing for a minute and listen or better yet ask your partner to hold their thought while you quickly finish what you are doing.

(178) Can you fall out of love? Yes, and it is possible to fall back in love. Do you know how many times we have fallen out of love with Jesus and we still go back? Sometimes you are highly motivated to serve God, sharing His works,

spending time in His presence, reading your scriptures, appreciating Him daily. Then suddenly you stopped for whatever reason you know and then six months later you go back to loving Him again by doing the same thing you used to do when you were in love with Him. The same is with the relationship you have with your partner. You can fall out of love when you stop loving, caring, appreciating, worshipping, and spending time with each other. And you can fall back in love by doing the aforementioned (loving, caring, spending time with each other, etc.)

(179)   If you are looking for a life partner, do not just look for someone that will cover you physically. But someone who will also fulfill the spiritual assignment in your life. The purpose of marriage is bigger than the two of you and your children.

(180)   The expectation of your new relationship is mostly hinged on the experience of your past relationship. You need to evaluate and heal from your experience so that you do not treat your current partner like your EX.

(181)   Sometimes your partner who hurts you did not even know what they did. And you are over there losing sleep. Listen, sleep is for PEACE and not for being PISSED. Perhaps you wish to hurt them so that they can feel what you feel, read this quote from Beyonce

that says, "Love is an endless act of forgiveness. Forgiveness is me giving up the right to hurt you for hurting me." Learn to forgive and move on with life quickly.

(182) Fight and issues often get unresolved in a relationship primarily because you are picking the wrong time to discuss it. Consult with your mate for a perfect time. Do not let your emotions, anger, and frustration dictate it.

(183) Not all the time sex requires foreplay. There are moments your partner does not want it and just desires direct action. It is advisable to read those moments and perhaps have such a discussion with your partner. Couples that talk about sex, experience increased satisfaction. Have sex dialogue with your partner; make it a habit.

(184) I know the relationship can be complicated. To unravel its complexity here is a simple formula approach: Know who you marry, Respect who you marry, Love who you marry, and Support who you marry.

(185) If there is no SACRIFICE, there is no LOVE. It is as simple as ABC. Sacrifice is giving up something in exchange or in demonstration for the greater love you have for your partner. If you love someone, you will make all the sacrifices to keep them.

(186) Ego does three things:
 (a) Protect your vulnerability, weakness, or fear
 (b) Prove that you are right, smart, or knowledgeable
 (c) Defend your statement, opinion, or partner.
If Ego is used in the wrong way, it can lead to an unhealthy relationship and hence divorce. Do not let your EGO drive you. Take control of it and let HUMILITY take charge.

(187) This is the mindset and what couples should tell each other instead of proving to be right to each other. "I'll rather tell you I'm sorry than proving to be right because I value you and our relationship more than being right.

(188) Every man becomes a baby around the right woman. No man is that strong that he cannot become tame. When he finds that special one, he lowers his guard. If your man is not your baby, then he is either not your man or you have not discovered what possibly could make him your baby.

(189) It is okay to naturally desire a compliment from another human being, but it is not okay to feel something must be wrong with you if you are not getting it. Believe that you are perfectly beautiful and attractive without a word of compliment from anyone.

(190)   Any man can change. He just needs to make up his mind to change, be touched by God, and do it for a good reason.

(191)   At times God does not want to communicate through a coach, counselor, or Pastor. He wants to communicate with you directly. So often we seek guidance from counselors, coaches, or pastors on relationship matters, but you are forgetting that they are not always going to be present and possibly not have the perfect answer. You need to start developing a personal relationship with God so you can hear directly what He's saying concerning who you marry. Some of the challenges you are facing can be solved with a single word from God directly to you.

(192)   If you are currently in a bad relationship, you can still build a brand new one with the same person who is willing to change. There is always a different season in a relationship just like you experience the different season in your own life. If you never gave up on yourself in those challenging personal seasons, then do not give up on the relationship with your spouse. With everyone committed to change and shifting things around, you can have the relationship you have always wanted.

(193)   You can treat the fruit of your problems but if you do not get to the root, the fruit will grow back. When you

experience the same problem re-occurring again after you have dealt with it so many times, it indicates that you have been addressing the fruit and not fixing the root. Nine out of ten relationship challenges people face are root problems that have grown and now bearing fruits. If you do not want the same fruit to keep growing again, you must get to the root of your problem and fix it.

(194) A relationship is an investment. If you do not invest in your relationship, it stands a chance of being stagnant or depreciating in love. It is imperative to sow quality time with your spouse, to understand each other more, expose each other to new things, introduce yourself to new ideas, and your relationship will become fun, healthy, and exciting.

(195) If you are having challenges or conflicts with your partner here are three important questions that can turn your relationship around for good! (a) What do you need that I am not giving you? (b) What would you like to hear from me that I have not said or would like me to say often? (c) What do you want me to show you that I need to? The answer to one or all these questions is the solutions, clue, or insight to what is missing. These questions speak about affection, provision, or attention, which are necessities in a relationship.

(196) Comparison is what people do in a relationship that does not realize is slowly killing their partner and hurting their relationship. If you must compare your partner to someone else to get them to do something or change, or as a parent you compare your children and cousins to each other, you already lost their interest to change. It creates more damage than what you are trying to fix in the first place. The best method is to consistently explain what you want them to do, and they will eventually change.

(197) If you can meet her emotional needs, it can increase her sexual drive.

(198) Don't deprive each other of sex. Are you and your partner having a big or any type of argument that is keeping y'all away from being intimate? Are you mad at your partner and using sex as a punishment? You are playing a dangerous game. Sex deprivation or starvation with your partner will create emotional withdraw that can make you feel lonely, moody, and ultimately break your intimate connection. It can also lead your partner to the hands of someone else if they do not have self-control.

(199) Men run your home in concert with your wife. It will not only give you peace of mind, but it will also make her feel part of the family. And you will have a thriv-

ing, healthy, happy, and high-performing family as a result. There is more to you and your partner than to you or your partner separately.

(200) Money is not everything, but it is necessary for building a relationship and a family.

(201) When your partner is secured and satisfied in the sex department, you will have enough drive, confidence, and glow to handle the work outside. Do not be so work or business-minded that you are forgetting to work with your partner who is the real work.

(202) Sex is an art; master it with your partner and do not be too eager to touch down! The journey is as important as the destination.

(203) If you are arguing, complains, and non-physical fight with your partner now and then does not mean your relationship is bad or you should break up. It should not stop you from loving one another as well. It just indicates that you guys still have more learning to do about each other. And it is better to learn than not to. Learning is part of your growth. If you are not learning, then you are not growing.

(204) Life is about the relationship. No one can make it without the help of another. Life is just designed that way. It is deemed important to know as well that a wrong

relationship will produce a bad result for you. It will slow you down or derail you from the right path to your goals. How can you know you are with the wrong person? The answer is in the following questions you ask yourself, "With this person in my life what do they have me thinking, feeling, doing, reading, saying, planning, where do they have me going? Am I progressing? If there is no positive answer and those answers do not align with your morals and Godly values, then you are in a relationship with the wrong person. When you are in a relationship with the wrong person, you end up where they are going.... not a good place.

(205) Are you in a relationship where there is an issue and the person reacted in a way that made you wonder what just happened? You noticed the issue is so minute, but the magnitude of their reaction is bigger than the issue itself. You start to question yourself what did I do wrong? Listen to me, you did not do anything wrong. They are not reacting to you. They are reacting based on the experience they had before with the person they had it with before you being in the picture. It is not you; it is them. You just triggered something that looks like their past situation. You are being treated by their wounds, their past, that they never dealt with and healed from. What you need to do is to have a dialogue with them where the reaction and attitude are coming

from. Who hurts them in the past? Is it their friend, ex, father, mother, or relatives? Get to the bottom of it and you will find answers.

(206) It is possible to rebuild your relationship after infidelity. You can get your love back, trust, respect, loyalty, and full commitment of your partner when they have been chattered due to infidelity. You do not have to get a divorce. According to divorce magazine, about 70% of couples stay together after an affair has been identified. Did you hear that? About 70% of couples stay together after an affair has been noticed. If those people can do it, I believe you are strong enough to do the same. You can still get back your old flame, love, respect, trust, and loyalty. Your relationship can even be stronger than what it was if only both parties are willing to do the work.

(207) Do not fight with someone you should be fighting for. The real offender is often the spirit behind the person. Most times you are fighting the wrong person. Do you think the arguments and the bad characters displayed often by your partner are mere their ignorance? The bible makes it clear, for we do not wrestle against flesh and blood, but principalities, against powers, against the rulers of the darkness of this age, against spiritual hosts of wickedness in the heavenly places. It is not just in your personal life, finances, and career

that you wrestle against principalities. In your marriage with your spouse, principalities are preventing your progress and unification. Evil thoughts are running through the minds of your partner to say or do things contrary to the standard and boundary of your relationship. I admonish you to take time to pray today and pray off every wrong idea and voice luring your partner to misbehave.

(208) Do your research very well before you jump into a new relationship. The grass is not always greener on the other side. Do not leave what you have for a 20 who looks like 80. It is called the 20/80 rule.

(209) 3 roles every man should play with his wife (a) Father: Protective and sensitive to your wife's environment and needs. Watch over her and guide her path (b) Husband: Act as a partner; you plan and strategize present and future goals together with your wife. Trade ideas and opinions that will move individual and family unit forward (c) Boyfriend: Fun and Wild. He is someone who does not take life too seriously. He explores and enjoys life together with his wife.

(210) Every right relationship should be able to bring you two things: Blessing and Lesson. If you are only getting one, then it is either you are not in the right relationship or you are not maximizing the relationship for what it

should be. You should be able to learn from your partner and at the same time be blessed by their presence in the relationship. It is like walking with God; we learn from our relationship with him and get blessed by him.

(211) Relationship Commandments Every Woman Should Know. These are irrefutable laws and commandments of relationship for women. When you break these principles, you break the heart of your man and possibly the relationship. (a) Do not correct your man publicly especially in front of his peers, family including his children, and known people. It is the highest order of disrespect and lack of wisdom on your part. Wait till you get in the car, at home, or in a private place to share your feelings or corrections. How people see you relate to your man is how they will relate with him. If you spoke to him anyhow, do not be surprised your friends, family or even strangers will address him improperly. (b) Do not speak anything negative about your partner to your family. It is not their place to know your partner's weakness and pain. Hide them; they are your private properties. When you divulge such private information, you have given your family power to influence your thinking and can lead to divorce. If you are sharing information about your man to your family to seek advice, kindly get a neutral person, a coach, counselor, or Pastor.

(212) Husbands make decisions that protect their wives and children regardless of what their parents/siblings think. Bible says Husband leave and cleave to your wife. A lot of men today are still not cleaving completely to their wives. They are being under the influence of their parents. You are doing a disservice to your partner whom you should be protecting and them finding security in you. What makes you a man is in decisions you make for your wife and children.

(213) When your partner is cranky kindly check first the sex activity before thinking of any other solution. Has s/he been fed lately, or it has been a minute? Sex is often the cure of a cranky partner.

(214) There is a threshold to what your partner can take. If you keep playing with their heart, they will just get up and leave you one day. Do right by your partner.

(215) Did you know you are responsible for 50% of the change in your relationship? You and your partner are designed to create the relationship you want and that means you have a part to play and so is your partner. Have you ever thought that your partner is not changing because there is no visual example of what they need to do and the result that will become the outcome of their action? But if you acted first and be the change you want to see, it can so happen that your action, pos-

itive energy, and the result can encourage your partner to step up to the plate. Therefore, do not wait for your partner to change first. You start the change. Do not wait for your partner to attend coaching, counseling, or workshop with you. Go without them. Do not wait for your partner to initiate sex. You do it first. Do not wait for them to apologize first, you go ahead and say sorry. Do not wait for them to greet you first. Let it be led by you.

(216) Appreciating your partner is a must! We need to appreciate each other in a relationship. What your partner does is not less valuable than what you do. You just have not seen their list of what they do. Pay attention very well to see what your partner does for you and the family and appreciate them for it. If it is paying bills, taking care of the kids, dropping them off in school, social activities, taking their baths, doing homework with them, doing laundry, making food, etc.

(217) Marriage is not a destination. It is a lifelong journey, and you must continually look for better ways to enjoy that ride with your spouse otherwise it will come to a halt.

(218) It is imperative to understand that in the construct of love relationships in modern-day society, there is no such thing as male roles or female roles. They are just

roles and whoever is gifted at the roles should perform them. What differentiates us and determines our roles is a gift, not our gender. It is our intrinsic interest, value, knowledge, capacity, and skill set we possess to perform the roles. Empowering each other as partners will spur economic growth, create power balance, increase everyone's self-happiness, and make you a better family.

(219) Your partner may not be the problem. It could be you. Could it be your attitude is what is hindering your relationship progress? A bad attitude is like a flat tire. It will get you nowhere. Check on your attitude and fix it.

(220) 7 THINGS YOU CAN DO WITH YOUR PARTNER AND CHILDREN:

(a) Work out together

(b) Rest more

(c) Read the bible and pray together as a family. The knowledge, spiritual strength, and covering you will receive can last you for a long time

(d) Play with the children. Take a walk with them and watch movies together at home

(e) Discuss family goals i.e. finances, projects, travels, activities, education, legacy, etc.

(f) Do house chores together as a family

(g) Become more romantic and intimate with your partner.

(221) Communication to your partner is not just talking. It involves having the right timing, a positive tone of voice, being kind, compassionate, showing empathy, and not being sarcastic.

(222) Do not stop spending time together as a couple. The danger of not spending quality time together with your partner is growing apart. Do not let your children, business, career, or third party come into your time together. The children will soon grow old and leave the house. Prioritize your time and find help from a nanny, family members, parents, or day-care.

(223) How do people feel about being around you? Especially your partner and children. Your personality or character is important. It can make people want to be around you or away from you. Are you someone your partner and family love to be around? Or there is peace, joy, and excitement when you are missing in action? Examine yourself.

(224) The argument is not worth losing your relationship over. Trying to win an argument can sometimes cause you to lose your relationship/partner. I believe the relationship is worth holding on to than the offense you are keeping. You either choose to be happy or to be right. Just saying "sorry" is sometimes all it takes to calm the tension and resolve the argument.

(225) Couples who are in the best relationship are not those without problems. They are the ones who work best with their problems.

(226) Your relationship needs spontaneity. One of the best things you can do to spice up your relationship is to be spontaneous. Do not let your relationship be routine and boring. By being spontaneous you have a way of surprising your partner, lifting their spirit, increasing their dopamine level, and drawing them to you. Find something spontaneous to do for your partner today.

(227) You cannot change a relationship. Really? Yea. you can only change the people living in the relationship. You need to understand that relationship is not an object you can modify. It is just a 'word' to describe people in a communal engagement. So, it is the people in the relationship that can bring about the change. If you change, then your relationship will reflect it.

(228) Anger can keep us from developing a spirit pleasing to God and our partner. Have you ever been proud that you did not strike out and say what was really on your mind to your partner? Self-control is good, but Christ wants us to practice thought-control as well. You cannot get to self-control if you have not fully executed thought-control effectively. Anger is a dangerous emotion to have that can threaten to leap out of control,

lead to violence, emotional hurt, and increased mental stress. Take control of your thought so that you can better handle your anger instead of your anger handling you.

(229) In a relationship, no one knows it all. There is always what you do not know that your partner knows. There is always what you lack that your partner has. This is one of the beauties of having a partner.

(230) Forgive your partner if you want your relationship to get better and last.

(231) Do not be intimidated if your partner is smarter in areas you are not and do not let that drive you to competition either. The relationship is designed to complement one another, not compete. It is a partnership you are forming, and in partnership, no one knows it all. Embrace and celebrate the competence of one another. Your relationship will thrive better when you do.

(232) Do not threaten to end a relationship with your partner to get him or her to do what you want. It is an unethical, immature, not biblical, and wrong approach that can frustrate your partner to give up. You may end up regretting it if the partner accepted the break-up. Talk through what you want, explain what you want, share how you feel about how he or she is treating you, and

get help. It is a better and safer method that could produce a better result than a threat.

(233) Every relationship is different and the secret to discovering what makes your relationship different is to learn how your partner is different. Stay away from comparing your relationship and partner with other people and forcing them to be who they are not.

(234) Communication is important. Women are typically communicative. Men are not. The times' men talk is to woo a woman, need sex or food. Lack of communication causes you and your partner to drift apart from each other. There can never be too much communication. The more you do, the better your relationship gets. It is important to talk and share your thoughts. Invite your woman into your world, what you are thinking, and plans you have either finished or still in the making. Let her offer you advice, seek her opinion, and strategize together. Two heads are better than one. The advantage of regular communication with your partner is that it brings you closer spiritually, emotionally, and mentally. It makes your partner feel inclusive, helps you understand each other, strengthens your bond and chemistry, solidifies your friendship, and helps you finish each other's thought because you have spent so much time conversing, now you understand how he or she thinks and the kind of decisions they can make in

a certain situation. Crawl out of your shell and have as much dialogue with your woman.

(235) You and your spouse do not talk the way you used to, and it may just seem like things are a little weird right now. But here is the real problem you are facing: If you do not reconnect now, statistics say there is a high probability that you will end up in a divorce. Even if you do not, you will live unhappily day-to-day, not with a lover, not with your best friend, but with a roommate. The only reason you are still staying together is for the kids or to pay the mortgage. I want you to make a switch today by engaging with your partner and addressing your issues. Identify games, activities, or trips you can take together that can facilitate the connection again.

(236) The modern-day approach to a successful marriage is the practice of relationship equity. To effectively execute it you must first understand the characteristics of a 21st-century woman you are in a relationship with. Who is a 21st-century woman? She got it together, money alone cannot please her. You must satisfy her mind, soul, and body. She got high expectations, she is resourceful, her place is more than the bedroom and kitchen, and she loves and thinks differently from your mum. If you understood this as a man, your approach to your woman will be to strike equity balance so that

you can maximize your family unit otherwise you will always be running into conflict and hence the divorce. What is relationship equity? Treating your partner the way you would like to be treated; being fair to each other, and determining roles based on skill set, gifting, constraints, and not gender.

(237) Has your value increased since you have gotten married? Has your worth to your partner been appreciated or depreciated? You must increase your worth and value in your home, business, career, etc. You should not be the same person your partner married. Life is about improvement. What can increase your worth? Your spiritual growth, financial growth, intelligence, knowledge, education, respect for your spouse, discipline, improved skill set, the spirit of submission/humility, team spirit, support, and involvement in the family.

(238) You are meant to cover each other as partners. There will be a trying time where money, education, wisdom, and knowledge that your partner possesses cannot solve the problem except prayers. There are issues you will run into in your life, marriage, family, ministry, career, business, health that the mundane things you have cannot solve except prayers. Get yourself a praying partner. Cultivate the habit to cover each other. A woman is made from a rib of her man. That rib covers the organs of the man. Likewise, the flesh of the man

covers the rib (his wife). You are meant to cover each other as partners.

(239) Love is not at its best when all is good between you and your partner. The true existence of love is demonstrated and revealed during adversity. You can only tell for sure if your partner loves you when there is a challenge. For example: If you are sick, does your partner show kindness to you by volunteering to run to the store to get you medication, prepare food for you to eat, or release you of chores so that you can rest? If you love your partner, are you willing to demonstrate it by going through coaching/counseling or workshop to get help so that you can be a better man or woman for your partner? Love is seen and tested in adversity. God did not demonstrate his love by sending Jesus when things were initially good in the garden. He did not send Jesus before the fall of men. He sent him when hell broke loose. When men's thoughts are full of evil. When men no longer respect the statutes of God. That is when He demonstrated his true love by sending his Son to reconcile us back to him, to set us back to the right path.

(240) If you and your partner are constantly on a separate page, eventually it can lead to divorce. The root cause of separation and divorce is due to two different minds working on two different plans. They want different things and cannot come to a unified agreement. If you

continue to operate like this with your partner and cannot decisively agree to be on one page, you will either become a roommate or get a divorce.

(241) A friend who has been married for over 20 years shared his secret sauce of holding the relationship together to be respectful, patient, finding ways to fall in love all over again, and not letting finance be the foundation of good or bad times. It is important to not let finances dictate the state of our relationship. That means you should not just celebrate that you made money but celebrate the foundation, the principles you followed with your partner that helped you to make the money. A principle such as having an agreement, a unified decision, and support to make the money. Don't just celebrate that you have a baby. Think of the principle you both followed such as creating time together to make love. Don't just celebrate that you finished school. Celebrate the time you put in, the sacrifice you made for each other during that tough time, helping each other with the chores while the other person could study. There is nothing wrong with celebrating result and making money but if you are always praising result and unfortunately the result does not come out the way you'd expected, you will be disappointed with each other, which will lead to unhappiness. However, when you celebrate the principles you followed, the partnership,

the understanding, team spirit, support, agreement & unification that you both executed during the journey, you will always be happy with each other regardless of if the result is good or bad.

(242) What is affecting your communication is that you are not allowing each other to speak. Study shows women speak ~30,000 and men speak ~1/3 of that. If you keep interrupting your woman in the middle of her talk, eventually she will carry over the rest till the following day and that will be a Psunami conversation at that point. Men, please let your woman finish expressing herself. She is built to speak and express herself.

(243) Do you get upset with what your partner says to you during an argument? This is a practical guide that can help you respond better: It is not what Tyffany says to James that matters; It is what James says to James that can help create a better response. Whenever your partner says something disrespectful to you or gets you upset, have an internal dialogue within yourself that is positive to 'counteract what you are being told by your partner.

(244) 91% of Dad-Kids bonding happens between age 0-12. A word of advice for men: Your children need you more for your presence than your performance. If you are always out to make money or putting more time to make

money so that you can "perform" and never present to give the children the value needed, your relationship with them will not grow deeper and your money for them may not be well spent. When you give them money and never have time to sit down and teach them the value of money or administer how they spend the money, they will possibly squander the money, which will push you out more to perform so that you can always replenish the money. Presence is much better than performance. There is a lot you can teach when you are present that you cannot teach from a distance. Balance both your performance and presence with your children.

(245) Are you having difficulty moving on from your past relationship? Are you still hurt by what the person did? Is your old relationship affecting the new one? Are you seeing patterns from your old relationship repeating in your new relationship? If yes, do you know why? Here is the reason: Though you left the relationship, however, all that relationship did not leave you especially if you were intimate and had a child together. It is like gluing two papers together. If you tried to separate them, some parts of each paper will be on the other part. You cannot fully separate the two papers without leaving a mark. You can change jobs and not feel any-

thing. You cannot change a serious relationship and not feel anything.

(246) The best relationship you can have is first with God than with yourself. If those two are not strong, then the one with your spouse will be weak.

(247) Your partner wants to be seen by you. Do you pay close attention to your partner? Do you observe and appreciate them for what they do, or you think it is just a task they are completing? Are you complimenting them for those tasks they are completing? It is important not to take what we do in the relationship for granted. They are not just tasks. We want to be seen, observed, appreciated, and complemented. Make sure you perform those things for your partner constantly.

(248) Spending quality time is a sign that shows someone is in love with you. People spend time with what or whom they love. If your partner is always making excuses of not spending time with you, trust me you are not their priority and there is no love with who you are not prioritizing.